AF482032

WEALTH BUILDING

through

HOMEOWNERSHIP

SABRINA GREEN

TABLE OF CONTENTS

INTRO

Elated, I took off running through every room of an empty house, screaming with joy yet crying happy tears. A moment in time that I will never forget! This moment was the day I received the keys to the home of my dreams. This one piece of monumental property became the best accomplishment I had ever endured for my family. I had grown up in one home, never understanding what it felt like to move. My mother had purchased a home when I was young, and I truly did not know that this feat for a single mother was a big achievement when I was younger.

I moved from home right after graduating from high school. By the time I graduated from college, I was a mother struggling to get by and moving every time my rent was raised. That rent notice became something like a crutch but also a signal I needed stability in my life. It wasn't until my son and I moved back to my parent's home that I realized I needed to make a change in my life. During this time, I started looking at model homes and dreaming of my future family being able to pack out this new home of ours. I dreamt of having 6 kids, and we would need a big house to fit comfortably, so I always planned to go big or go home when it came to the house I'd like.

Well into my career, I decided to see if I could get approved to purchase a home that took my breath away. It was that day I walked out of that office, defeated with a huge denial. My debt was too high, and my credit was too low. I personally thought my dream was no longer achievable. I would forever move all my housing items from place to place, spending so much every year to keep my housing costs the same. Feeling powerless, I went back to the one person who now had three homes and plenty of history with purchasing homes, my mom. What she taught me is what I will be laying out for you all. The importance of being prepared before you go purchase a home and knowing more about the home buying process. Needless to say, I took the time to raise my credit score on my own over four months and honed in on what was holding me back before. It also took a major financial change to save some funds for my down payment, but it all paid off after two offers were turned down and the last offer was accepted. Outlined in this text you will find an extensive amount of information about the process of purchasing a home, and I hope that the journey is all worth it in the end for you and your family to have a place of your own to call home.

Everyone's story is different. Your motivation may not look like my motivation. Your background is not identical to my experience, but what is the same are our desires.

Homeownership is a goal for millions of parents across the globe. It gives you a sense of ownership, stability, and belonging. Just the simple thought of not having to move or ask permission to decorate was motivation enough for me! With homeownership, you gain the comfort of building your family legacy that can be passed down from generation to generation and building wealth that can be leveraged for decades to come.

One of my main messages with compiling this book is to help more people, hard-working parents, and all alike, build wealth through homeownership.

Within this text, I will lay out the process of not only becoming a homeowner but also the preparation needed to make sure you get the best loan, rates, monthly payments, and down payment assistance to be able to effectively purchase your dream home. My goal is to help you know you are getting the most bang for your buck and confirmation that through any economic changes, your foundation will continue to be grounded.

REALITY OF CREDIT

Your credit report shows your personal credit history of data submitted by creditors to the credit bureaus. While we have so much more information to dive into regarding homeownership, we are starting here because I feel this is the first task for you to review and start working on immediately. The lower your credit score, the harder it is to get qualified for loan programs and better rates that will help you with purchasing your home.

It is thought that credit bureaus have a legal responsibility to report accurate information, but the reality is it's up to you to make sure the information is correct. The credit bureaus are data collectors, and each month they receive millions of pieces of credit data, so it's no wonder there is a high rate of errors being reported.

The most frequently used credit-scoring system, known as FICO, uses a formula developed by Fair, Isaacs, and Co. Scores range from 300 to 900 points, with higher numbers denoting a better credit rating. According to Fair, Isaacs,

Co., the score is calculated weighing different aspects of your credit history and behavior in the following manner:

- 35 percent represents your bill-paying history.

- 30 percent represents your level of outstanding debt.

- 15 percent represents the length of your credit history.

- 10 percent represents a combination of your credit accounts and loans.

- 10 percent represents your applications for new credit (a high number of applications in a short space of time generally leads to a lower score).

As a credit connoisseur, I have to let you know that it does take time to build up your credit if it is low, but there are ways to raise your score quickly with advanced tactics. It is highly suggested to be in the high 600's or even in the 700's when purchasing your home. Your credit score could be the deciding factor of paying thousands of extra dollars. I will show you exactly how in later topics but for the time being, go to <u>AccelYourCredit.com</u> and book a free consultation with me to get action steps to raise your score.

Improvement of your credit can be done on your own and offer quick credit score updates. It is proven that when you build positive credit items and use your credit wisely, the older negative information has less of an impact. Below are some steps you can take today to help increase your score:

Pay all your bills on time.

- This is the most crucial action you can take to improve your credit report. Also, try to pay more than the minimum required payment. Mail-in your payments at least seven days before the due date to ensure your creditors receive them on time. •

Keep your debt level low.

- Set a goal to keep your non-mortgage debt payments less than 20 percent of your take-home pay. Credit grantors don't always take a positive view of you having lots of credit cards with high credit limits even if you don't use them. We suggest you apply for reasonable credit limits and keep your debts well below your credit limits.

Correct inaccurate information as soon as possible.

- If you notice that any information on your credit report is wrong, contact the credit reporting bureaus as soon as you can to correct the information. This applies to accounts that are yours but report differently across the 3 credit bureaus. You can leverage the FCRA law that states inaccurate information has to be deleted. Once you send the letter to the credit bureaus, they have to respond with validation of the account or delete it entirely.

Make sure you have open credit card accounts.

- When verifying your credit report, you should have at least one open revolving card reporting. The lack of any open credit means you are missing out on credit points and also not showing you can correctly handle a credit account responsibly. If you run into not being approved, I have a list of cards you can get with now hard inquiry pull along with card options that give people with low scores guaranteed approval. Please feel free to reach out to those at credit@legacymym.com.

Raise your credit limits on current open cards.

- Outstanding debt is 30% of your score, and raising your credit limit on open cards changes the ratio of your credit profile. Asking for a credit increase may make a good point change for your profile just by adding more credit. It is crucial that you practice good credit habits and do not use the new credit limit but pay down any outstanding balances on each card.

Verifying your credit through the process of becoming application ready will help you stay on top of where you currently are and also help you gauge when is a good time to apply as your credit increases. Before you move on, make the commitment to verify where you currently stand with your credit so during this process, you can mark a high credit score off your to do list.

MONEY PROVIDES THE MOVES

Homeownership is one of the biggest purchases parents typically make their entire lives! It's a commitment for sure and not one to take lightly. It is also not a task that lenders take lightly either. What your realtor and lender will not do is sit you down and determine what you really can afford in your everyday life compared to what you can afford on paper. On paper, they are bringing in your gross income and calculating a percentage for you to stay under, but your real-life needs could be a totally different makeup. Your lender is concerned about how to get you qualified for a loan while the realtor is consumed with finding you a home that meets your needs and within your approval limits. You, on the other hand, need to take in your household and what is within your budget.

Unless you have the cash on hand to purchase a $100,000 house or more outright, then you will need financing to make this dream a reality. A lender is a bank or financial backer of your loan. This is where your money will be coming from and who you will be paying monthly for the life of your mortgage loan. Your lender will have a series of requirements and forms to be completed. They have to verify that you are stable and able to repay back the funds they will give you. I have a breakdown of what they typically request and how you can get prepared, but we are going to start with the basics! Where the money is, so we know what type of moves you can make.

To start this task of determining where the money is at requires you to create a budget for your household. A budget is the tracking of your income and expenses so you can see:

1. What are you spending monthly?
2. Determine any financial changes you need to make to reach a goal.
3. Control your spending.
4. Plan for large purchases.
5. Save for retirement or build an emergency fund.

What we use it for is to verify your new home purchase fits your current budget. Extra expenses will happen with your home purchase, so it is always a good idea to know where you currently are in your finances. Your budget can be an estimate of monthly income and expenses, but actual amounts will be even better to track. We customized a budget template for you here: http://bit.ly/LFSbudget. This is the document I currently use, and it does all the calculations for you. Within my 90 to Homeowners course, we dig deeper into each person's budget to detail where they can save and also ways to build up their emergency fund; and if you would like to help yourself, please send over a copy of your completed budget to help@legacymym.com, and I can speak with you directly.

What we don't want to happen is what is called being "home broke." When you go apply for a mortgage loan, the lender is going to approve you for a fixed amount. For example, let's say you get approved for $350,000, and at that rate, your monthly payment would be $1,700 monthly. Just because you're approved for that amount doesn't mean that you should purchase in that range. A few things to look at are what you are comfortable with and what your budget allows. If you are renting at $900 a month, what type of adjustments do you need to make, if any, to know how to pay the new monthly rate? Also, you should work the new monthly amount into your budget to see where your new monthly totals will be. It is all about preparing for this new adjustment, and the more you know, the better prepared you are long term if anything surprises happen. So, in essence, house broke means you have no additional funds in your budget due to the monthly cost of your home maxing out your budget.

It is a good financial tactic to always know what your budget is, especially for big, long term purchases.

Additional Budget items First time Home Owners overlook:

Maintenance costs
HOA dues
Utilities
Mortgage Insurance
Homeowners insurance
Property taxes
Landscaping/yard work
Hvac system costs
Pest control

Getting a home warranty that covers numerous things not normally underwritten by home insurance can help off-set the costs of unexpected repairs. In some cases, the seller may be willing to pay for the warranty when you buy the home.

CALCULATE YOUR JOURNEY

To know that you understand what your budget looks like, you need to take a look at how the bank views if you get a loan and how much you qualify for. The lender works with the bank or funding company to determine if you can afford a mortgage. To do this, they calculate your debt to income ratio (DTI). This looks into how much of your income is needed to pay your debt obligations like your mortgage, student loans, credit cards, and car payments. Most lenders typically want no more than 36% of your gross income to be going towards your monthly debt. Within that, they look to have your mortgage payment to be no more than 28% of that calculation. For parents whose DTI is over that amount, there may be exceptions depending on your lender. Still, typically you would need to lower your monthly expenses, avoid any new debt, or bring in more income to meet the monthly percentage terms.

You can use your DTI to see what the value of homes is within your affordability. It also gives the lenders reassurance that they will collect their money back and you won't foreclose on the home. Calculating your DTI starts with knowing your monthly income. If there is more than one person on the loan, use both incomes along with all debts combined.

"Then take the total and multiply it first by 0.28, and then by 0.36, or 0.43 if you're angling for a qualified mortgage. For example, if you and your spouse have a combined gross monthly income of $7,000:

- **$7,000 x 0.28 = $1,960**
- **$7,000 x 0.36 = $2,520**
- **$7,000 x 0.43 = $3,101**

This means that your mortgage, taxes, and insurance payments can't exceed $1,960 per month, and your total monthly debt payments should be no more than $2,520, mortgage payment included.

Unfortunately, you need to keep your monthly payments under both of these limits. So the next step is to see what effect your other debts have. Add up your total monthly non-mortgage debt payments, such as monthly credit card or car payments.

For this example, we will assume your monthly debt payments come to $950. Computing the maximum mortgage payment:

- **$2,520 - $950 = $1,570**

Since you have relatively high non-mortgage debt in this example, you're limited to spending $1,570 on a mortgage, taxes, and insurance for a new home. If, on the other hand, you had only $500 in non-mortgage monthly debt payments, you could spend the full $1,960 on your home since $1,960 + $500 = $2,460 (or less than your overall monthly payment limit of $2,520)." Thebalance.com

Insider Tip: You can calculate what your buying power is by using a mortgage calculator! To this before you continue by dialing in on the estimated monthly toolbar. Check out this mortgage calculator https://legacyfs.kartra.com/page/Mortgcalc I also created a short video on using the mortgage calculator. View video here (link to a video uploaded on youtube page)

HOMEBUYING PROCESS

We often hear that the journey to homeownership is a simple process: Complete the application, look for a home, go through escrow, and you are now a homeowner!

If it were that easy, everyone would have a home, and most apartments would be non-existent. Face it, who likes having neighbors stomping upstairs, or someone raises your rent and tells you not to hang your television on the wall? No one, that is who. The path to homeownership is a list of items that need to be completed, but it is not linear. There are subcategories that go in-depth, and while it may seem like it's simple, there is so much more going on to complete each task.

Before we go into more detail, I want to review the people involved in the home buying process and their functions.

Loan Officer:	A financial professional who will determine approximately how much money you'll be able to borrow for a mortgage loan.
Mortgage Lender:	The business person or financial institution that provides the money you'll use to purchase your new home.
Mortgage Broker:	An individual or organization that brings together mortgage lenders and borrowers.
Loan Servicer:	An organization that handles the day-to-day management (i.e., collecting, billing, and record-keeping) of your loan.
Real Estate Agents, Brokers, and Realtors	Trained professionals who are licensed to negotiate the sale and purchase of real estate.
Home Seller:	The property owner who puts a home up for sale.
Home Inspector:	An individual who provides a trained, professional opinion of the physical condition of a home and its components and systems.
Home Appraiser:	An individual who provides a trained, professional opinion of the market value of a home.

Insurance Agent:	A financial professional who provides protection against the risk of monetary loss.
Title Company:	A company that examines public records to determine that property rights can legally be transferred from one owner to another.

You have done your work to get your credit right and also understand how much house you can afford to buy based on your budget. While using the mortgage calculator, you should now get more of an understanding of what you can afford to buy. Don't worry about your down payment amount was not much. We will be covering some tricks to get more for your down payment and closing costs.

LOAN TYPES

Every loan is different and non created the same. It is imperative to know the type of loan that fits you. Some loans have little fluctuations during the life of the loan, while others may change every 3-4 years. It is critical that you pick the right loan based on your needs. I highly suggest a fixed loan because the rate you start with is what you will have locked in for the remainder of the loan, but I do want to show you the variations there are so you can choose for yourself. It is best to consult with your real estate team to explore your best options.

FHA Loans - Government-backed loan that helps make homeownership possible for borrowers who don't have a large down payment saved up and may not have a strong credit score. You'll need a minimum credit score of 580 if you wish to go with the minimum 3.5% down payment, which is lower when compared to traditional mortgages.

Fixed or Adjustable-Rate Loans: If you plan to stay in your home for at least 7-10 years, a fixed-rate mortgage offers stability with your monthly payments. If you don't plan to stay in your home beyond a few years, an adjustable-rate mortgage could help you save big on interest payments. One thing to note is if you lived through the Great Recession (which is presumably everyone reading this article), the term Adjustable Rate Mortgage (ARM) might cause flashbacks to a day when your 401k was plummeting, and you were laid off work, your parents severely cut your allowance money, or worse. ARMs were indeed a major cause of the housing market crash in late 2007. Something to note, however, is that it wasn't the existence of ARMs that caused the problem; it was that the wrong people were obtaining them at their lender's guidance.

Jumbo Loans - It makes sense for wealthier buyers purchasing a home above the conforming loan limits. Borrowers should have good to excellent credit, high incomes, and a substantial down payment.

Conventional Loans - Ideal for borrowers with strong credit, a stable income and employment history, and a down payment of at least three percent.

The credit score varies with each lender on the credit score needed, but it is typically around 640 to apply for a conventional loan, and the down payments start as low as 3%.

VA Loans - Government-backed loan that provides flexibility, low-interest mortgages for members of the U.S. military (active duty and veterans). VA loans do not require a down payment or PMI.

USDA Loans - Government-backed loan that helps moderate to low income borrowers purchase a home in a designated for rural development USDA-eligible area. You must meet certain income limits to qualify. Some USDA loans do not require a down payment for eligible borrowers with low income.

INTEREST RATES

Your interest rate is the long-term cost of your loan, and the origination is the upfront cost. It is a highly variable expense over which your lender has control and is not the same across the board. Your credit score determines your interest rate during the time of your application: the higher your credit score, the lower your interest rate. With the purchase of a home typically being fifteen to thirty years, your interest rate being as low as you can get it can save you thousands of dollars over the life of your loan. That is one reason we started working on credit first, but If you need help raising your score, book a free consultation with me to see how we can help at AccelYourCredit.com. Just because one company gives you one rate doesn't mean that the next lender does not have a lower rate. Below is a comparison of rates of the years so you can get a better understanding of how a rate can affect your monthly payment.

MORE BUYING POWER

"As of mid-July, the monthly mortgage payment on the average-priced home purchase, is $1,071 which is down 6% from the same time last year. In fact, buying power is now up 10% year-over-year, meaning the average home buyer can afford nearly $32,000 more home than they could at the same time last year, while keeping their monthly payment the same."

MORTGAGE RATES BY DECADE FOR A $300,000 HOME

1970s	8.86%	$2,384
1980s	12.7%	$3,248
1990s	8.12%	$2,267
2000s	6.29%	$1,855
2010s	4.09%	$1,448
TODAY	2.96%	$1,250

What the graphic above does not cover is the total interest paid over the life of the 30 loans for 4.09% = $222,234.83 while the total at 2.96% = $153,742.54. What this shows us is that with the lower interest rate, a buyer could save $68,492.29 over the life of the loan with these new interest rates. This, in turn, now qualifies buyers for a higher-priced house since the rates are at historical lows.

The higher the interest rate, the higher your monthly payment, and vise versa. Current interest rates are one of the reasons behind the writing of this information. The economy today has historically low mortgage rates, and although we are in a pandemic, it is still a great time to work on purchasing a home if your criteria fits.

FINDING THE BEST LOAN

Lenders are not one size fits all. You can shop around to find the lender who gives you the best deal on rates. To determine your costs, you would be required to complete a loan application and submit documentation for them to provide you with the loan estimate.

When shopping for a mortgage, there is no use securing a low-interest rate if you have to pay an enormous origination charge in exchange. When comparing one loan against another, be sure to include this factor in your calculations. There will be advertisements that try to lure you in. We're all familiar with the typical promotions from our local car dealership: "Zero Down!" "Sign and Drive!" "No Credit, No Problem!" and a whole host of teaser loan options. What we may not realize is that these high-risk loan options are often not in our best interest. From a bank's perspective, lending is a risk/reward calculation, meaning that the higher the risk associated with your loan, the more money you'll be charged over the long term. Along with higher costs for not either having good credit or having no down payment, there are also origination fees that can be astronomical! But with shopping around, you will be able to see all the differences from one lender to the next. When you get at least two loan estimates, you can compare your best options before committing to a lender. Below are some criteria to review to help you determine how much each lender will differ.

Things to consider:

- Loan features - prepayment penalty, balloon payment
- Loan Program - Conventional, FHA loans, VA loans, Jumbo loans
- Fixed vs. Adjustable - Rates are fixed vs. Rates are adjustable
- Term - Length of the loan and rates with each
- Mortgage Insurance - Additional costs for the loan type
- Buydown or credits - buy down for lower rates
- Comparing interest rates - expressed as Interest rate or as Annual percentage rate(APR)

Taking the list above into consideration, follow these steps to find out which company is providing the better deal.

1. Get a "loan estimate" for both offers
2. Determine the difference between the monthly payments (a)
3. Calculate the difference between the closing costs (b)
4. Find the break-even point (c)

   The break-even point refers to the amount of time it takes to recoup the initial cost of buying a lower interest rate. To calculate this, take the difference in total loan costs (b), divided by the difference in monthly payment (a), divided by 12 months. The result is the number of years it will take to recoup your investment (c). Usually, the break-even point on a rate buydown is between 5 and 10 years.

Equation: b/a/12=c

5. Choosing your loan

Shopping around helps you get the best deals when purchasing a home. Overall, finding the break-even point is necessary to help you save a good chunk of change! The APR is calculated over the full term of your loan (i.e., APR on a 30 year fixed average all loan costs over 30-years). It is rare that homeowners carry a loan for a full 30 years without refinancing or selling their home. There are a ton of reasons one might refinance their mortgage, from seeking a better interest rate to changing their term, to consolidating credit card debt, to buying a new boat.

So, let's say your break-even point is 8 years, and to do this loan, you are paying more to buy down the loan to the interest rate according to the loan estimate. If you choose to buy down your interest rate, you are betting that you will not refinance or sell until after you reach the break-even point (8 years). If you decide to change, refinance, or sell before then, you will have paid all that money upfront, never to recoup it in the long run. On the flip side, you might opt for the lender credit, assuming that you will move soon or that interest rates will go lower in the future. If things don't work out the way you plan, though, you'll be stuck indefinitely with an interest rate that could be higher than necessary.

This is a really easy way to make sure your loan aligns with your personal expectations and budget. Plus, doing the work upfront set you up to have no surprises later down the road. Although expectations may, and usually do, change down the road, all we can do is plan for now and make sure we can handle the changes in the future as they come. Shopping around will give you leverage to a better deal and overall, save you more money.

DOWN PAYMENT VS. CLOSING COSTS

When looking into purchasing a home, there will be downpayment percentages that you will see with different types of loans you have to choose from. The down payment is the upfront cash you pay to get a home loan, and it's expressed as a percentage of the home price. The required down payment depends on the type of mortgage and the lender. The first two parts of the downpayment is the earnest money, or cash used to start escrow when you make your initial offer on the home. The second part is the remainder of the down payment, which is given to the lender when you close the home.

Closing costs cover fees, taxes, and administrative expenses required to process the purchase of your home, while your down payment usually consists of two parts. The first part of the down payment is the earnest money or the cash you put in escrow when you first make an "offer to purchase" on the home.

What I want to clarify is that these two payments make up two separate roles in the transaction. Even though you have the down payment, you will still need to come up with the closing costs. The closing costs do not include the down payment. Don't worry; I will lay out ways to cover these costs later. Any funds you put down will be deducted from the purchase price of the house. So with the variations of loan types, your down payment is typically tied to the percentage of the home price. For FHA loans, the required down payment is 3.5%. To calculate the down payment, you would take the cost of the house and times it by the down payment percentage. In this case, let's determine the down payment for a $300,000 loan. 300,000 x 3.5% = $10,500 down. The higher the percentage, the more money you have to come up with out of pocket.

Closing costs are the costs to cover the expenses to complete the loan. This assortment of taxes and fees are dependent on the type of loan you have, but on occasion, you can get these costs added to the loan. You can expect your closing costs to be about 2% - 3% of your purchase price. The closing costs do not reduce the purchase price when paid and are due at the closing of escrow.

I have attached a loan estimate for you to look over. For some, all the information is scary, but this is your way to know exactly what you are paying for during your home purchase. While some of these costs have to do with the mortgage, many do not. These costs are broken down in detail on the second page of the loan estimate (LE), which all mortgage lenders are required by law to provide before accepting deposits.

Loan Costs

A. Origination Charges	**$1,802**
.25 % of Loan Amount (Points)	$405
Application Fee	$300
Underwriting Fee	$1,097
B. Services You Cannot Shop For	**$672**
Appraisal Fee	$405
Credit Report Fee	$30
Flood Determination Fee	$20
Flood Monitoring Fee	$32
Tax Monitoring Fee	$75
Tax Status Research Fee	$110
C. Services You Can Shop For	**$3,198**
Pest Inspection Fee	$135
Survey Fee	$65
Title – Insurance Binder	$700
Title – Lender's Title Policy	$535
Title – Settlement Agent Fee	$502
Title – Title Search	$1,261
D. TOTAL LOAN COSTS (A + B + C)	**$5,672**

Other Costs

E. Taxes and Other Government Fees		**$85**
Recording Fees and Other Taxes		$85
Transfer Taxes		
F. Prepaids		**$867**
Homeowner's Insurance Premium (6 months)		$605
Mortgage Insurance Premium (months)		
Prepaid Interest ($17.44 per day for 15 days @ 3.875%)		$262
Property Taxes (months)		
G. Initial Escrow Payment at Closing		**$413**
Homeowner's Insurance	$100.83 per month for 2 mo.	$202
Mortgage Insurance	per month for mo.	
Property Taxes	$105.30 per month for 2 mo.	$211
H. Other		**$1,017**
Title – Owner's Title Policy (optional)		$1,017
I. TOTAL OTHER COSTS (E + F + G + H)		**$2,382**
J. TOTAL CLOSING COSTS		**$8,054**
D + I		$8,054
Lender Credits		

Calculating Cash to Close

Total Closing Costs (J)	$8,054
Closing Costs Financed (Paid from your Loan Amount)	$0
Down Payment/Funds from Borrower	$18,000
Deposit	– $10,000
Funds for Borrower	$0
Seller Credits	$0
Adjustments and Other Credits	$0
Estimated Cash to Close	**$16,054**

Calculating Cash to Close

Total Closing Costs (J)	$8,054	← Addition of all fees calculated above
Closing Costs Financed (Paid from your Loan Amount)	$0	
Down Payment/Funds from Borrower	$18,000	← Initial down payment amount
Deposit	– $10,000	← Amount deposited as earnest money
Funds for Borrower	$0	
Seller Credits	$0	
Adjustments and Other Credits	$0	
Estimated Cash to Close	$16,054	← Total amount left to be paid at closing

HOW TO GET A DOWN PAYMENT AND CLOSING FUNDS

Now that you understand more about the loan types, what down payment percentages look like for each, along with how to calculate the amount you need to work towards, let's dive into where the money will come from! There are a variety of ways to come up with the costs to purchase a home. By knowing your budget and purchasing range, you can better determine how much you can afford to buy. You are also now able to determine what your down payment will range along with the closing costs of your proposed loan. This helps you determine the amount you need to bring to the table. My goal is for you to be confident in knowing what is going on and knowing what to expect. I've personally had clients cry to me how they felt when they were denied a home loan and also feeling defeated because they had no clue what amount they would have to pay to purchase. Not having a down payment or money needed to purchase a home has been one of the top two reasons I have seen people hold off from buying a home. Some completely through the ideal of homeownership out the window, but it doesn't have to be that way. So let's strategize what you can get the money from.

Start Saving Now

Every penny counts! From your budget, if you can start putting money away every month, it doesn't hurt to have it available for your home purchase. What I have had clients do is automate their savings. To do this, they open a savings account, preferably a high yield savings account, and set up for a certain amount of their wages to automatically be transferred over to this account every paycheck. This amount does not have to be substantial, but it does have to be done automatically. This cuts down on you seeing the funds, and creates an account that can build on autopilot.

Find programs that Help

Your lender would be the person to ask about programs in your area, but if they do not know, you can also find them yourself. Here are some popular searches you can go deeper into to see if there are available programs in your area that you may qualify for.

1. First-time homebuyer assistance in (enter your city)

2. https://www.hud.gov/states/ Look into homeownership assistance by your state to see what programs are available. This site will also show you which lenders are approved to offer the FHA loans and can be a great place to start.

3. Check with the Federal Housing Administration (FHA) and Veteran's Affairs (VA). Both of these bodies have home loan programs for individuals, and some have a down payment component. You can also find assistance options by consulting with your state on the Department of Housing or Urban Development websites.

4. Neighborhood Stabilization Program (NSP) or neighborhood assistance housing program.

5. You may qualify for down payment assistance if you're an educator, healthcare worker, firefighter, police officer, or another type of civic employee. If you're a first-time homebuyer or haven't owned a home in more than three years (re-qualifying you as a first-time buyer), you could also qualify for down payment help.

6. Search homeownership assistance in (your city, and your county)

LEVERAGE YOUR TAX RETURN

One of the easiest ways to get or start building your downpayment for your home is if you receive a yearly tax refund. This lump sum can literally be used as the down payment for your future. Putting all or majority of your refund away can be an advantage to acquire funds quicker.

Gifts

Gift money from relatives or friends can provide a big boost. The money must be an outright gift and not a loan. The rules for gift money vary by loan program. In some cases, you may be required to contribute some of your own cash in addition to the gift money.

Seller Concessions

A seller concession is a credit proved by the seller of the home to be used toward closing costs. Seller concessions can be used to pay for closing costs only, not a down payment. This is something you can talk to your realtor about as a tactic to help you purchase the home with less money needed at closing. Another seller concession could also be applied after the home inspection. The total of the repairs the seller agrees to pay for can also be applied to your closing costs to lower the amount of your down payment. Seller concessions can be used to pay for closing costs only, not down payment.

Lender Credits

A lender credit can be used to cover closing costs, but not down payment. A lender credit can either be created by the lender waiving standard fees or by using premium pricing to generate a rebate. Consult your lender to determine if this would work for you.

Those are just some of the ways you can go about getting your down payment and closing costs secured to purchase your dream home, but please take the time to hire a professional. I can not tell you how having people in your corner through this process can really help you get through it all. One misstep on your part or just a failed piece of paperwork can delay your closing or possibly ruin your chances of getting the home.

- What First Time Home Buyers Need to Know

- Not every lender is approved to offer the program

- Down payment assistance varies by State and also by City

- Most popular Assistance programs

- Closing cost can be paid by the seller

THE APPLICATION

Congratulations! By doing the homework above and making sure you are within the limits described, and you have just preapproved yourself! Now it is time to prepare for the application process. At this point, you can either work with your realtor, who will put you in contact with a mortgage lender or loan officer. The loan officer is your source of completing the application to determine if you meet the requirements to purchase, and they will also let you know how much you may qualify for. It is highly recommended to get pre-qualified before you start viewing homes. There are three main factors that will make or break your application approval are 1. Length of employment 2. Credit score 3. Debt to income ratio.

I want to note: Lenders all have different lending requirements, all are not approved to offer first time home buyers programs, and they also have different fees that you need to know upfront. So, I've comprised a list of questions you can ask your lender before they take your application or run your credit. I definitely want you to know that you are in control and they will be working for you. If you don't feel comfortable with your loan officer or even your realtor, please find one that you like.

Questions to ask loan officer:

- ▶ How much can I borrow?

- ▶ How much of a down payment will I need?

- ▶ What is the interest rate?

- ▶ Will my loan be fixed?

- ▶ Do you qualify for any down payment assistance programs?

- ▶ What would my interest rate be?

- ▶ What are my estimated closing costs?

- ▶ How often will I be updated on the loan's progress?

- ▶ What is the typical length of escrow?

- ▶ It is crucial to understand that the lender will have to run your credit to determine where you stand with rates and also approval status. If you aren't completely ready, which sometimes happens, you can ask for a prequalification letter. Prequalification means you have provided the lender with an overview of your information, but it has not been verified.

A pre-approval letter is when the lender has gone more in-depth to confirm at least some of your financial information and credit. With this process of pre-approval you will formally be submitting a loan application. As stated above, every lender is different when it comes to the documentation they need to pre-approve you for a loan. Be ready to supply some, if not all, of the documentation listed below.

1. Last 3 months of pay stubs
2. Last 2 years of tax returns
3. W-2's or 1099's
4. Other income documentation
5. Bank statements
6. History of mortgage or rent payments
7. Identification

Insider Tip: Use the information that you can prove or document. Overstating income that is unverifiable will change your pre-approval amounts. Speak with the lender regarding forms of employment that are not verifiable.

Most lenders can get you a pre-approval letter once this information is received. By law, the lender must send you a loan estimate within three business days of receiving the loan application. A loan estimate gives you more detailed specifications of your loan terms. It is a snapshot of the proposed terms. It lays out estimations of the interest rate, monthly payment, tax and insurance costs, potential penalties, and closing costs.

After this process is complete, you officially know how much you qualify for and can begin your search of homes in your desired price range. Please note, just because you were qualified for a certain amount does not mean that you have to get that amount. It is always best to review your budget and personal goals to determine what works best for you and your family.

Looking for the home you love, a neighborhood you see your family in, and that overall dream home can be quick or even drawn out. Your realtors' job is to help you determine what you like and narrow down your dream home. Their role in this process is to guide you not only with finding a good home but to also educate you and keep the process of escrow smooth and stress-free. There are no upfront fees to hire a realtor, but there will be a commission that is applied during your closing costs that they collect once your loan closes.

Times have changed over the last decade, and most realtors require that you have a pre-approval before going out to look for homes. It helps them stay within your budget and narrow down the process. But, to be clear: any pre-approval letter, whether it's a prequalification, pre-approval, or full upfront financial underwrite, is *not* considered a commitment to lend. There are several scenarios where your mortgage can fall through, even after receiving a fully-underwritten pre-approval.

ESCROW - CONDITIONAL REPORTS

Before we get into the do's and don'ts of escrow let's go through how exciting the term "I'm in Escrow!" really is.

An escrow company is a neutral third party that handles all of the terms of the purchase agreement and monies for deposits to the transaction. Once you find the home of your dreams and make an offer, the seller can either accept your offer, counter your offer, or deny your offer. Escrow happens once your offer has been accepted, and the purchase agreement is signed by both parties. This officially starts the process of the house being purchased by you! This is also the time that the lender will start verifying your application and making sure everything you stated is true and correct so they can finalize your loan.

Once you enter escrow, you will be asked to deposit an "earnest money" amount into escrow. That means it isn't going directly to the seller but is being held by an impartial third party until you and the seller negotiate a contract and close the deal. You can't touch it, and the seller can't touch it. It's in escrow. This money is held as a good faith deposit, and these funds can be forfeited if you do not hold up your side of the bargain with purchasing the house. Say you change your mind at the last minute and decide you don't want to purchase the house; your earnest money can be given to the seller for backing out of the purchase.

I need to define a *contingency period*. This is a period built into the beginning of the escrow process when one party or the other can walk away without consequences or penalty, usually for a specific reason. For instance, the default on the standard forms here in California is that all offers to purchase are *contingent* upon the loan for seventeen calendar days after acceptance. It is best to know the contingency period within your state and ask your team what is the contingency date for your loan once you enter escrow.

Escrow is held by a title company that is like a middle man for the transaction. Documentation and signing go through the title company, and once they have all approvals and documentation, they release funds and titles to the necessary parties, also known as "closing escrow."

Conditional reports during escrow are requested from your lender. This process is called "underwriting," and the underwriter will typically have a list of documents that you will have to supply for them to prove you are qualified for the loan. Submitting documentation in a timely manner will help escrow move along smoothly. If you fail to provide the needed documentation, it could cause you to "fall out of escrow," meaning you are not approved for the loan.

Here are some examples of deals that may fall out of escrow:

The appraisal value is not met.
The buyer cannot get full loan approval
Home inspections reveals serious issues with the house
Borrower make a purchase that make them disqualified
    for the loan
Issues with the title

Failure of the buyer to qualify for financing is by far the most common reason for escrow failure. This means that something goes astray with the buyer's quest to acquire necessary financing. They cannot qualify for the loan, and they do not qualify within the escrow period under the contract. Due to changes in lending law and practices, it's now taking a minimum of 45 days for loans, but a loan officer could typically get the loan done in thirty days.

Another big reason loans fall out of escrow is because borrowers make changes in their financial lives that disqualify them. During escrow, it is crucial that you do not add any new lines of credit, use any credit, allow any negative items to hit your credit, go on a shopping spree, large deposits to your checking account, or make purchases that can affect your credit. Another thing to note is changing or losing your job can also change things with escrow. So for the duration of escrow, you need to keep everything in your life, and credit matters exactly how it was when you started escrow. The underwriter does random checks during the process to verify that you still are working along with a credit check towards the end of escrow to verify your credit hasn't dropped significantly, and no big changes were made. So, wait! Wait for the new car purchase, the new furniture purchase, wait until you have the keys to your new home in your hand before you make any changes to what you originally reported. You risk losing your loan and, in return, your home if you do not follow these instructions.

ESCROW - INSPECTIONS

Once escrow has started, the contingency period starts. During that time, you will need to learn as much as you can to make sure you are getting a home that meets your qualifications. During this time, your realtor should have the appraisal completed and the home inspections done. The appraisal is the unbiased professional evaluation of the home and used to determine whether the home's contract price is appropriate given the home's condition, location, and features. In a refinance transaction, an appraisal assures the lender that it isn't handing the borrower more money than the home is worth. The borrower usually pays for the appraisal, and if the value is lower than expected, the transaction can be delayed or canceled. Home inspections focus on the home's current condition. Once the home inspection is completed, the report is submitted for the buyer to view the assessment. The report can include everything from material defects that may negatively impact a home's value to cosmetic defects, which don't affect safety or functionality. From this report, a buyer may decide to proceed with the sale, schedule additional inspections, renegotiate the sale price with the homeowner (if there are serious issues), ask that certain repairs be made, or cancel the contract. If the buyer requests major repairs, they may also ask for a reinspection with the original inspector to verify that the original problem identified has been remedied. Other infections that can be completed are pest inspections, termite inspections, and environmental inspections.

ESCROW - INSURANCES

Lenders may require that your new home have a title report and insurance. Since companies can put liens against your home loan if you fail to fulfill an obligation, this insurance is to protect the new buyer and lender against any unforeseen liens that may surface from the seller. Hazard insurance is another coverage required in some areas and is a homeowners policy that is added to the escrow of your loan. This policy is paid through your escrow account and the company selected to ensure you, and monthly payments are made through your mortgage payments and escrow account.

ESCROW - PROPERTY TAXES

You will have the choice to include your property taxes into your mortgage payment. Property taxes are paid twice yearly for the land your home sits on. These payments change based on land values. Your lender will estimate your monthly payment, including the principal and interest, and also the estimated monthly escrow payment (which goes towards property taxes and homeowners insurance) based on a typical home in the area where you're looking to buy. Property taxes combined in your mortgage will be the reason there may be slight fluctuations year to year with your loan payments. One year your payment could go up by $50 a month, and the next, it could go down $50 a month. It depends on your city, and the evaluation of land from year to year. Although your monthly payment would be lower if you remove the taxes and insurance held in escrow it is important to say that adjusting to having this payment in your mortgage saves headaches of making them on time. Non-payment of your property taxes can lead to your home being sold in a tax sale.

CLOSING OF ESCROW

During the last stages of escrow, you should definitely do a final walkthrough of the property, although at this point, you won't be able to back out. This is just to check that no new damage has happened to the home, and items specified in the purchase agreement are still left. One day before closing, you will receive the final loan statement and closing costs. This form should be compared to your good faith estimate you signed prior. Look out for excessive fees. While the closing process varies somewhat by state, you'll need to sign a ton of paperwork. This will take some time but don't rush, make sure you take your time and read carefully. The seller will have papers to sign as well. After all the papers are signed, the escrow officer will prepare a new deed naming you as the property's owner and send it to the county recorder. You'll submit a cashier's check or arrange a wire transfer to meet the remaining down payment, some of which is covered by your earnest money. Your lender will wire your loan funds to escrow so the seller and, if applicable, the seller's lender can be paid.

This is where the celebration comes in! You have completed the process of purchasing a home for your family to make memories for many years to come! I cannot begin to explain how happy I will be for you once you apply the information you have read up to this point. I'd personally love to see you online in your new home so make sure you tag me in your story for a special housewarming treat.

BUILDING WEALTH

Being locked into your new home offers benefits that can help you in your future if needed. Wealth building through homeownership is a tactic that has been used for centuries! I want to break this down for you by starting with the definition of wealth.

Wealth is "an abundance of valuable possessions or money." What does the word "wealth" mean to you? Most consider it a form of being rich, but here we are going to speak in terms of having leverage. Your new home can now be leveraged.

Your leverage starts the day you start paying your mortgage. That monthly rent payment from before is now benefiting you. These monthly mortgage payments are paying down the loan on your home. Over time, even with the fluctuations in the economy, the value of your home typically appreciates, which means it will "rise in value or price." So the home you bought for $200,000 will eventually go higher and can be sold for more than you bought it for. This is building equity. Equity is "the money value of a property or of an interest in a property in excess of claims or liens against it." In essence, the value of the home minus the amount you owe is the equity you have in your property. The value of the home can fluctuate, but statistics show homeownership is a smart choice. This amount can be borrowed against, refinanced, and withdrawn, purchase other properties, finance other purchases, pay down current debt, etcetera. Consider this forced savings.

Example:

Home Market Value | $280,000
Mortgage Owed | $145,000
Your Home Equity | $135,000

If you sold the home at the market value, you would have $135,000.

Another thing to note is this home can now be passed down through your family. It offers a place to call home and build memories for generations to come. For your children, it could also be a form of passive income if they decide to rent the home out. Also, down the road, it could be a home that you've invested in that pays you out if you decide to sell and reinvest in another home somewhere else. The possibilities are endless for your family to benefit from the investment you are making.

In conclusion, this information should be a guide for you to prepare yourself for the journey towards being a homeowner. I hope that this eases your mind about the process and shows you how to make your dream a reality but also arms you to know how to protect yourself during the process. My prayers are with every reader of this book. Blessings to you and yours.